Flying B

Elena Martin

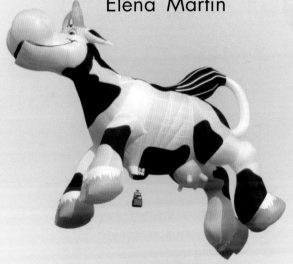

Rigby®

A Harcourt Achieve Imprint

www.Rigby.com
1-800-531-5015

The big rainbow balloon
is flying in the sky!

The big football balloon
is flying in the sky!

5

The big flag balloon
is flying in the sky!

The big sun balloon
is flying in the sky!

9

The big bee balloon
is flying in the sky.

The big cow balloon
is flying in the sky.

The big dinosaur balloon
is flying in the sky!

I am flying in the sky!